Quotations from Vice Chairman
Lán Àidí

哈这个篮子里什么都没有

[product]

Beverly ∘ Seattle ∘ Bellagio

First Official CPC Edition 1960-10-1 by 安静的人出版社,
No.2, 2nd Donghuan Road, 10th Yousong Ind. Dist.,
Longhua, Baoan, Shenzhen City, Guangdong Province, P.R. China 518109

First English Edition 1974-06-16 by LÁN ÀIDÍ Preservation Society, Ltd.
46 Park Rd, London NW8 7RG, United Kingdom

1

THE SILENT INSPIRATION
OF LÁN ÀIDÍ

Crafted from the collective spirit of the proletariat, Lán Àidí (Basket
Eddy) emerged as a paragon of socialist virtue during the tumultuous
years of China's Cultural Revolution. Born from the fiery crucible of
revolutionary fervor, his form embodied the aspirations of the working
class, molded by the hands of artisans dedicated to the cause of proletarian liberation.[1]

The rise of Lán Àidí to prominence was swift and decisive, as he quick-
ly garnered the attention of Chairman Mao with his unwavering and
stalwart commitment to the principles of Marxism-Leninism. Elevated
to the esteemed position of second-in-command in the venerated Gang
of Four by Jiang Qing, Lán Àidí became a stalwart defender of the
revolution[2], his rigid countenance a testament to the indomitable will
of the proletariat.

On the battlefield of revolutionary struggle, the Vice Chairman van-
quished all those who dared to oppose the righteous march of socialism.
With unwavering determination, he led the charge against counter-rev-
olutionary elements, rooting out bourgeois influences with unyielding

fervor. His steadfast dedication to the cause inspired legions of workers and peasants to rise up against their oppressors, forging a path towards a new socialist utopia.

Throughout the trials and tribulations of the Cultural Revolution, Lán Àidí remained an unflinching symbol of proletarian resolve. Clad in the emblematic red armband of the revolution, he stood as a beacon of hope for the oppressed masses, his silent vigilance a constant reminder of the inevitability of proletarian victory.

Though the winds of change have long since swept through the corridors of power, the Vice Chairman's legacy endures as a testament to the enduring spirit of socialism. In the annals of history, he remains immortalized as a champion of the people, his name forever synonymous with the triumph of the proletarian revolution.

These are his words. Read them. Learn them. Grind them up in the crucible of your struggles and steep them in the tea of your illustrious sorrows. Use them in your quest to vanquish your fears, to remain steadfast in your battles, and yet stay refreshed. Best served with an earnest serving of mountain honey over ice.[3]

[1] At Jiang Qing's insistence, all prior mentions of Lán Àidí were cleansed from the official records after she enrolled him into the Gang of Four. We are left to scrui-

tinize his past through the documented words Madame Mao spoke when the Vice Chairman was inducted as Grandmaster of the Ancient Order of the Purple Haze. In 1967, Lán Àidí mysteriously disappeared from the People's Republic of China after he was escorted by Premier Zhou Enlai to the Central Investigation Department (CID) for a meeting with the Eight Bureau, known later as the Institute of Contemporary International Relations.

[2] Vice Chairman of the Communist Party of China, Vice Chairman of the Central Committee of the Communist Party of China, Vice Chairman of the People's Republic of China, Marshal of the People's Republic of China, Watcher of the Skies, Sash Bearer of the Red House, Grandmaster of the Ancient Order of the Purple Haze, Commander of the People's Liberation Huángsè de Submarine Fleet.

[3] From Mao Zedong's most popular pamphet of 1934, *Preparing Tea for The Long March*.

ILLUSTRATIONS

1. 让哲学成为群众的利器 *(Ràng zhéxué chéngwéi qúnzhòng de lìqì/Let Philosophy Become A Sharp Weapon To The People)*, c. 1967-9, CCP mass-produced poster.

2. 日，國慶日 *(Guóqìngrì/National Celebration Day) Parade*, 1963, 人民日报 (Rénmín Rìbào/The People's Daily) photograph.

3. 不做资本主义走狗的傀儡 *(Bù zuò zìběn zhǔyì zǒugǒu de kuǐlěi/Don't Be A Dummy Against The Capitalist Running Dogs)*, c. 1966, Re-education poster created by The Ministry of Education of the People's Republic of China.

4. 大力支持农业 *(Dàlì zhīchí nóngyè/Strong Support For Agriculture)*, c. 1964, COPCO Seed package insert.

从这里开始

52

请立即停止

大力支援农业

革命武器库中最重要的武器——虽然不是由钢铁锻造的，却具有切穿敌人谎言和欺骗的力量。这种武器就是语言。在我们争取解放和正义的斗争中，语言不仅仅是声音或符号；它们是刺穿反动和帝国主义心脏的矛。

在我们踏上中国未来之路的风浪中，我们不仅在战场上面对挑战，还在思想领域面临考验。反动势力，无论是国内的还是国外的，都会利用他们的宣传像毒药一样，试图破坏我们的事业，歪曲我们的目标。他们散布关于我们意图的谎言，诋毁我们的领导人，并试图在群众中挑拨离间。

同志们，我们必须用我们的语言来教育和提升群众。每一次演讲，每一份宣传单，每一篇文章都是可以穿透无知和误导盔甲的矛。我们的干部必须深入群众，倾听他们的关切，与他们心连心。我们必须使用能够引起工人和农民日常斗争共鸣的简单语言，这种语言能够激励行动并在实现更美好未来的可能性上增强信心。

此外，我们不必害怕敌人的言辞。他们的宣传反映了他们的绝望和虚弱。他们知道人民的事业是正义的，历史站在我们这一边。他们喊得越大声，越是表明他们害怕我们日益增长的力量。让他们抛出谎言；我们将以真理作答，坦率而大胆地讲出真相。用正确的言辞，我们自己的言辞，斩断反革命分子谎言和欺骗的线。

坚持我们的道路。不要成为他们的傀儡。

署名篮爱迪

《致农民》，1964年左右，COPCO 种子包装插页文本.

The most vital weapon in our revolutionary arsenal—a weapon that, while not forged of steel, possesses the power to cut through the lies and deceptions of our enemies. This weapon is the word. In our struggle for liberation and justice, words are not mere sounds or symbols; they are spears that pierce the heart of reaction and imperialism.

As we navigate the turbulent waters of China's path toward the future, we face challenges not only on the battlefield but in the realm of ideas. The reactionary forces, both domestic and foreign, wield their propaganda like poison, seeking to undermine our cause and distort our purpose. They spread lies about our intentions, slander our leaders, and try to sow discord among the masses.

Comrades, we must use our words to educate and uplift the masses. Every speech, every pamphlet, every article is a spear that can penetrate the armor of ignorance and misinformation. Our cadres must go among the people, listen to their concerns, and speak to their hearts. We must use simple language that resonates with the everyday struggles of workers and peasants, language that inspires action and instills confidence in the possibility of a better future.

Moreover, we must not fear the words of our enemies. Their propaganda is a reflection of their desperation and weakness. They know that the people's cause is just and that history is on our side. The louder they shout, the more they reveal their fear of our growing strength. Let them hurl their lies; we will counter with the truth, spoken plainly and boldly. Use the right words, our own words, to cut through the strings of lies and deceit of the counter-revolutionaries.

Stay the course. Don't become their puppet.

Signed, Lán Àidí

To The Farmers, c. 1964, COPCO Seed package insert text.